1. The West Maui mountains and Haleakala peeking through the clouds.

2. The view of Kaanapali Beach from the Sheraton Maui Hotel

4. Kaanapali Beach with the island of Lanai in the background.

5. Aerial view of Olowalu along the road to Lahaina.

6. Hibiscus, the Hawaii State Flower.

8. Fleming's Beach with Honolua Bay in the background.

10. Kahakuloa village on sleepy West Maui.

11. The exotic flower, Bird of Paradise.

12. Kaahumanu Church, completed in this form in 1876.

14. The steep walls of Iao Valley after a rain.

15. The Iao Needle and Iao stream.

17. Haleakala Crater, the House of the Sun.

18. Cactus and lantana blooms on the slopes of Haleakala in the Kula district.

19. Hookipa, Maui, is windsurfing country extraordinaire.

21. Wailua Falls, Hana, Maui.

23. The black sand beach at Wainapanapa.

24. Sunrise over Hana Bay.

25. The gray sands of Hamoa Beach.

27. Kaupo Ranch and Kaupo Gap.

29. Wailea Beach on Maui's south shore.

30. Morning sun over Maalaea Bay.

31. A Maui sunset.